COMPOSER PORTRAITS

Richard Rodney Bennett

His life *&* work *with authoritative* text *and* selected music

T0056684

Published by
WISE PUBLICATIONS
14-15 Berners Street, London W1T 3LJ, UK.

Exclusive Distributors:

MUSIC SALES LIMITED
Distribution Centre, Newmarket Road,
Bury St Edmunds, Suffolk IP33 3YB, UK.

MUSIC SALES CORPORATION
180 Madison Avenue, 24th Floor,
New York NY 10016, USA.

MUSIC SALES PTY LIMITED
Units 3-4, 17 Willfox Street, Condell Park,
NSW 2200, Australia.

Order No. AM1007886
ISBN: 978-1-78305-382-7
This book © Copyright 2014 Wise Publications,
a division of Music Sales Limited.

Edited by Sam Lung.
Biography and introductory texts by Anthony Meredith.
Music engraved and processed by Elius Gravure Musicale
and Paul Ewers Music Design.
Cover design by Chloe Alexander.

Printed in the EU.

WISE PUBLICATIONS
London / New York / Paris / Sydney / Copenhagen / Berlin / Madrid / Hong Kong / Tokyo

Richard Rodney Bennett

'the complete musician'

RICHARD'S parents were both musical. His father was briefly an opera singer and his mother, a fine pianist, was Gustav Holst's pupil at the Royal College of Music. Scores abounded in their Budleigh Salterton home — not least Chopin and the French impressionists — and there was a good piano to which the young Richard was irresistibly drawn. At 5 he was not only playing Debussy with aplomb but extemporizing. 'I didn't ever decide I was going to be a composer,' he would say later. 'It was like being tall. It's what I was. It's what I did.'

In adolescence he rebelled against his parents' conservative tastes, and by the time he was studying at the Royal Academy of Music with Lennox Berkeley and Howard Ferguson he was already a protégé of Elisabeth Lutyens, making annual pilgrimages to Darmstadt and Dartington, well versed in serial complexities. Disappointed by the Academy's pre-occupation with the past, he formed a New Music Society with a few friends, and in one concert he and Cornelius Cardew, after many months of study, gave the British première of Boulez's formidable first book of *Structures*. He later performed the equally formidable First Piano Sonata before the composer himself and, aided by a scholarship, successfully applied to become his pupil for a year. And so, at 20, he left the Academy without taking any exams and headed for Paris. The die seemed cast: his life would be devoted to the avant-garde.

But he had already written a score as a 19-year-old for a big feature film, *Interpol* (starring Victor Mature), which was released in Paris in 1956 while he was there. And on his return to London he started a double life, writing tunefully for the cinema while steadily developing his own unorthodox and distinctively attractive serial style. Likewise, as a professional pianist, he combined the light jazz he played at occasional gigs with regular avant-garde concerts (often with accomplished partners like Susan Bradshaw, Malcolm Williamson and Jane Manning).

Both of his double lives flourished, but their balance shifted significantly in the mid-Seventies, when a new career, as a singer-pianist exploring and reinterpreting the Great American Songbook, signalled his retirement as a performer of classical music. There was another shift in the Eighties, when in the wake of his move from London to New York his two lives moved closer as he edged his way back to tonality, leading to major works like the Third Symphony, *Concerto for Stan Getz*, *Partita* and *Reflections on a Scottish Folk Song*. He finally bequeathed a catalogue of over 70 scores for film and TV and 300 other commissioned works of diverse genres and consistently skilful craftsmanship.

Richard Rodney Bennett was arguably the most complete musician of his time; his expertise at the keyboard, which gave so much pleasure to cabaret audiences over nearly forty years, running parallel throughout his life with a compositional flair that seemed to know no bounds. Both great gifts are exemplified in this wide-ranging collection of piano pieces.

Anthony Meredith
January 2014

Tango After Syrinx

ICHARD once likened composition to mining. It was important, he said, to extract the maximum from a good seam. One such seam, inspiring several fine chamber works, was Debussy's flute solo celebrating the Greek nymph Syrinx (who, in scorning the lecherous Pan, provided him, through a rash metamorphosis, with reeds for his pipe). When, therefore, Richard was asked for a tango by the American pianist-composer Yvar-Emilian Mikhashoff (a university professor from Buffalo), the lovely nymph again beckoned enticingly.

Tango After Syrinx is an admirable example of Richard's ability to invest the discords of twelve-tone music with a beguiling and lustrous sensuality. Indeed, with the ghostly shadows of Debussy billowing around to exotic Latin-American rhythms, it is surely as inspired an improvisation as the original *Syrinx*. It was a perfect extrovert showpiece for Mikhashoff (originally Ronald Mackay) who clearly liked the big gesture and whose own compositions included arresting titles like 'Sergei Prokofiev sees penguins in front of his house and writes a concerto' and 'Francis Poulenc makes a daring escape from the Keystone cops'. It was one of 127 tangos Mikhashoff elicited from composers from over 30 countries and he gave it its premiere in New York City in one of his awesome tango marathons.

For Yvar Mikhashoff

Tango After Syrinx

Richard Rodney Bennett

New York City,
Dec 16th, 1985

Eustace And Hilda

EUSTACE *And Hilda* was a three-part television dramatisation of a trilogy of novels by L.P. Hartley, screened on BBC2 with a cast that included Flora Robson, Susan Fleetwood, Billie Whitelaw, Tim Pigott-Smith and Edward Hardwicke. It tells of an intensely loving relationship between a brother and his sister in the shifting fortunes of childhood and adult life. 'In any age and by any standard,' wrote the distinguished critic David Cecil, 'Hartley's book would be a masterpiece. Eustace's story has a complex, bittersweet charm, playful and pensive, humorous and fantastic, tender and mysterious.'

The short piano version of the main theme, though somewhat dwarfed by Richard's original orchestral score that helped sustain three and a half hours of screen drama, still reveals how unerringly Richard captured the essence of the story's mood, its dreamy protagonist Eustace, its upper-class social background and its period, either side of the First World War. In a few bars of the theme's final statement we even have a hint of Eustace's domineering elder sister, Hilda, and, in the dying chords, the underlying sadness of the novels — all the bewilderment and heart-ache engendered by human inability to rise above its weaknesses and attain its lofty ideals.

Eustace And Hilda
(Theme)

Richard Rodney Bennett

poco rit.   a tempo

poco rit.   a tempo   rit.

Impromptu on the name of Haydn

THE BBC has always been good on anniversaries, and Radio 3 gallantly played non-stop Haydn on the last day of March 1982 to celebrate the 250th anniversary of his birth. Back in 1909, on the centenary of his death, six French composers (Debussy, Ravel, Dukas, Widor, d'Indy and Hahn) had been asked to contribute pieces to a short *Hommage à Haydn*, an idea that the BBC copied, commissioning six British composers for a new act of homage: Richard, George Benjamin, Lennox Berkeley, Robert Sherlaw Johnson, John McCabe and Edmund Rubbra. This project, which specifically requested that the pieces be based on the pitches from the accepted musical transliteration of Haydn's name (BADDG), duly received a performance by John McCabe (who had earlier in the day played the *Hommage*) in a discreet late-night programme of just 15 minutes.

Richard's passionate contribution, expertly crafted and glittering brightly with a flowing accompaniment to the main melody, both as first introduced and later as inverted, beautifully conveys an impromptu's essential feeling of extemporization. John McCabe, writing of Haydn at the time of this anniversary, praised 'his depth of expression and mastery of a huge variety of genres'. The same could apply to Richard.

Impromptu on the name of Haydn

Richard Rodney Bennett

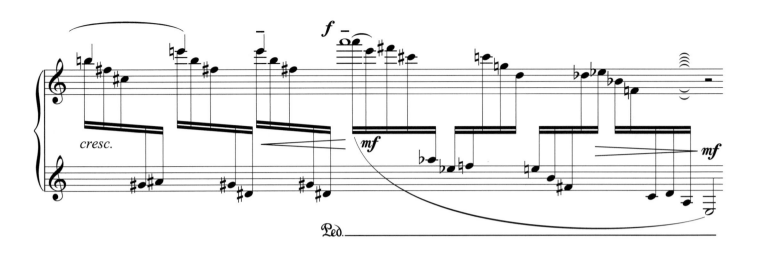

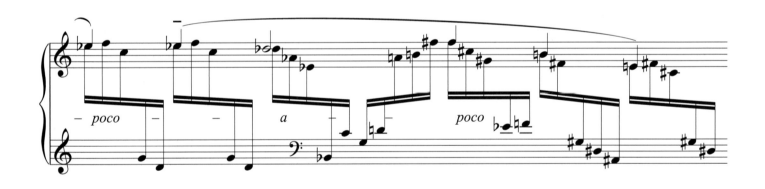

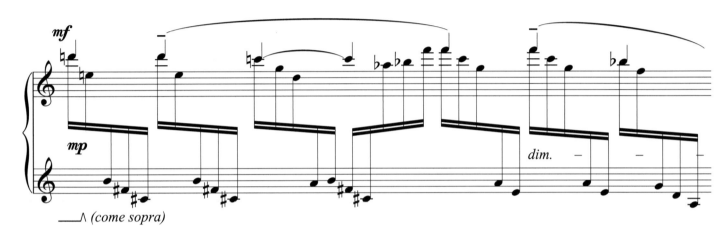

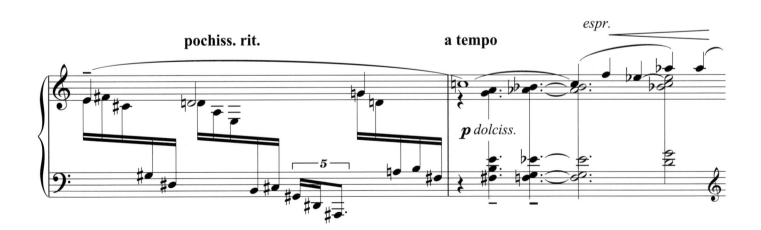

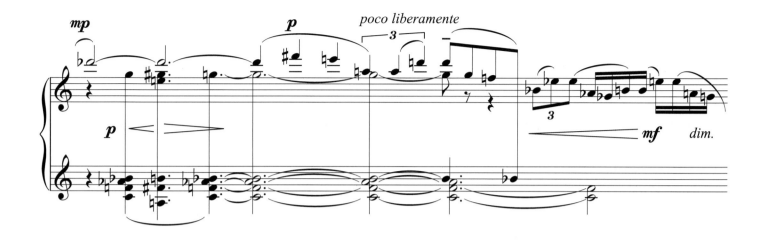

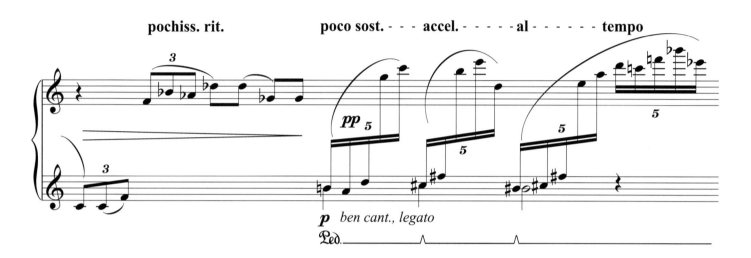

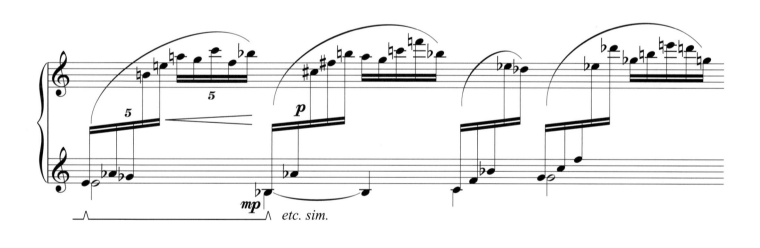

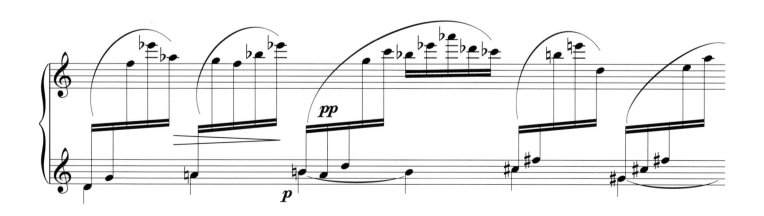

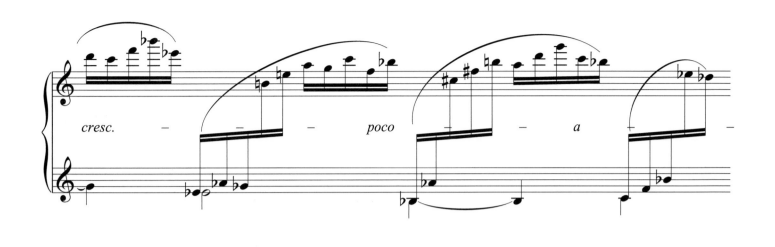

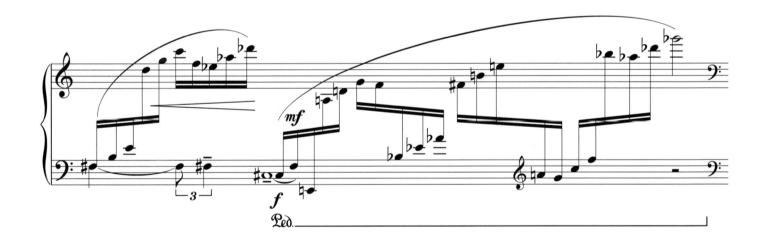

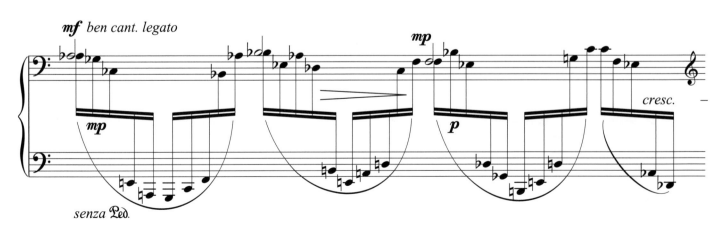

16

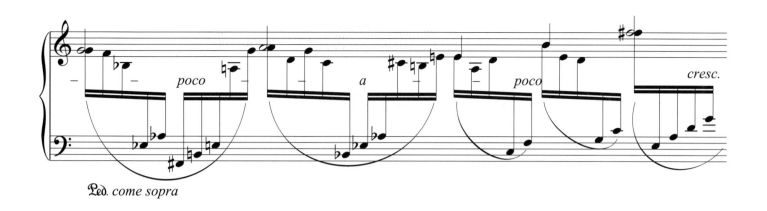

poco a poco cresc.

Ped. come sopra

pochiss. rit.   **a tempo**

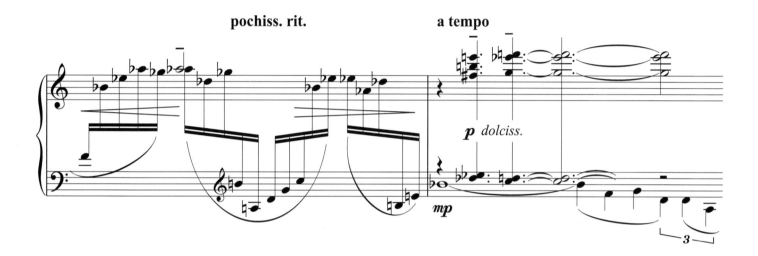

p dolciss.

mp

3

Poco sost., tranquillo

(R.H.)

p

p   5

pp   3

3

Ped.

poco rit.   **Lento** (♩ = 66)

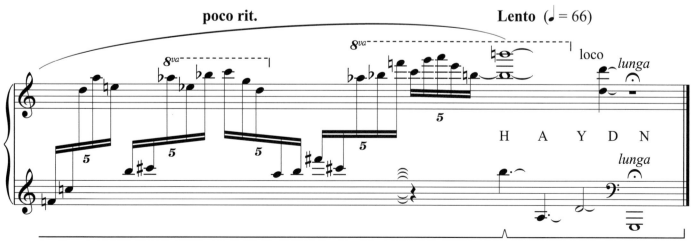

8va

loco

lunga

H A Y D N

lunga

5   5   5   5   5

Rosemary's Waltz

from Tender Is The Night

IT may have been helpful to Richard that at the time he was involved in the BBC2 6-part serialisation of Scott Fitzgerald's saga of the jazz age and the ultra-rich, *Tender Is The Night*, he was performing with Marion Montgomery at London's Ritz Hotel. At all events he had fun integrating many original jazzy recordings into some key pieces of his own (with the ondes Martenot very much to the fore). He later made two delightful piano works from these key pieces.

A charming foxtrot, 'Nicole's Theme', is both a portrait of Nicole herself (a rich but mentally unstable beauty who marries her hospital doctor, Dick Diver) and a hint of the smart milieu on the French Riviera in the 1920s which would ultimately destroy him. Similarly, the bittersweet 'Rosemary's Waltz' alludes to both the loveliness of the young film star Rosemary Hoyt and the unhappy consequences that her capricious pursuit of Diver will have. 'Rosemary's Waltz' is just a delicate miniature and yet the intricate tracery of Richard's melodic gift has the same flowing invention as some beautifully carved architectural detail in a Gothic cathedral. 'It's almost promiscuous,' he once admitted with a smile, 'inventing ideas which are both fascinating and thrilling!'

Rosemary's Waltz

from Tender Is The Night

Richard Rodney Bennett

a tempo, con moto

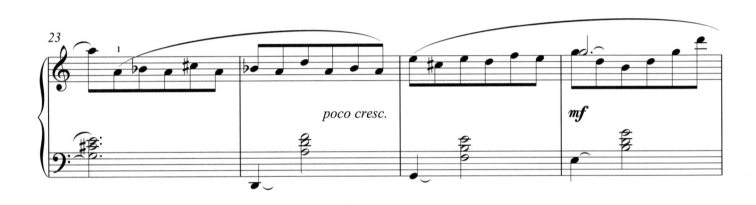

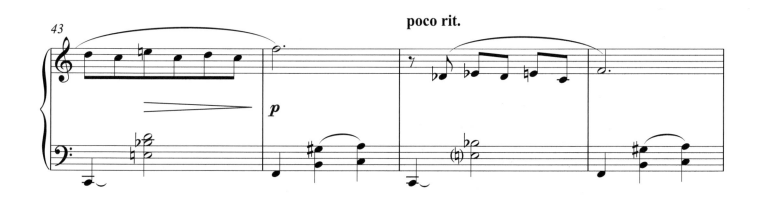

21

Three Romantic Pieces

III. Andante semplice

RICHARD was always grateful for the support and friendship of his composition teacher at the Academy, Howard Ferguson, who proudly boasted he had never passed a single exam, yet was described by the BBC on his 80th birthday as 'the compleat musician: composer, pianist, teacher and scholar'. Among several works commissioned in honour of that birthday were Richard's *Three Romantic Pieces*, which Clifford Benson played in a live concert from Pebble Mill that also featured Ferguson's own violin sonatas. Richard, on top form, would seem to be mischievously demonstrating to his old tutor that contemporary music, with its deliberate dissonances, can nonetheless abound in the vitality and emotion that Ferguson himself preferred to find in earlier centuries.

The deeply moving last movement, Andante semplice, shows Richard characteristically weaving complex creations out of tiny threads. ('I'm very economical with material. If I have a motif, I love to make nineteen different ideas from it.') The motif in question relates to another seam that Richard had been working: a ballad by Harold Arlen, 'I Had Myself A True Love', specifically used in the Andante of his Sonata for Soprano Saxophone and Piano and probably subconsciously in his Third Symphony. Johnny Mercer's lyric had a special personal relevance for him.

For Howard Ferguson on his 80th birthday, with love and gratitude

Three Romantic Pieces

III. Andante semplice

Richard Rodney Bennett

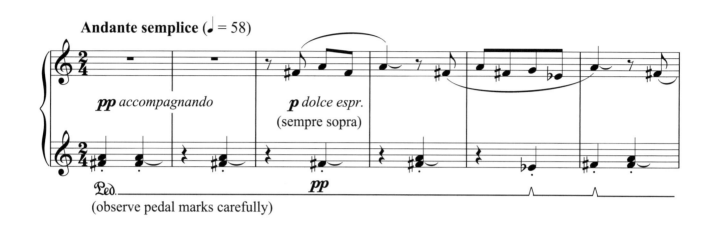

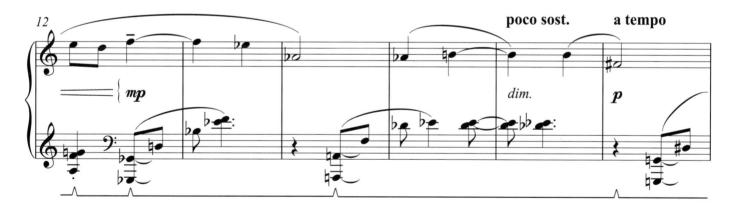

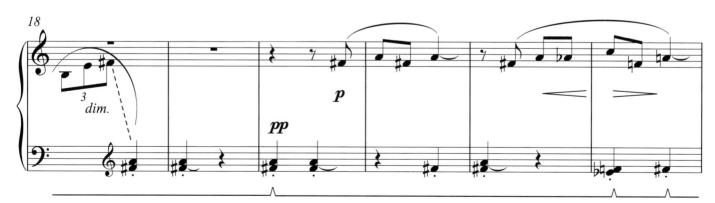

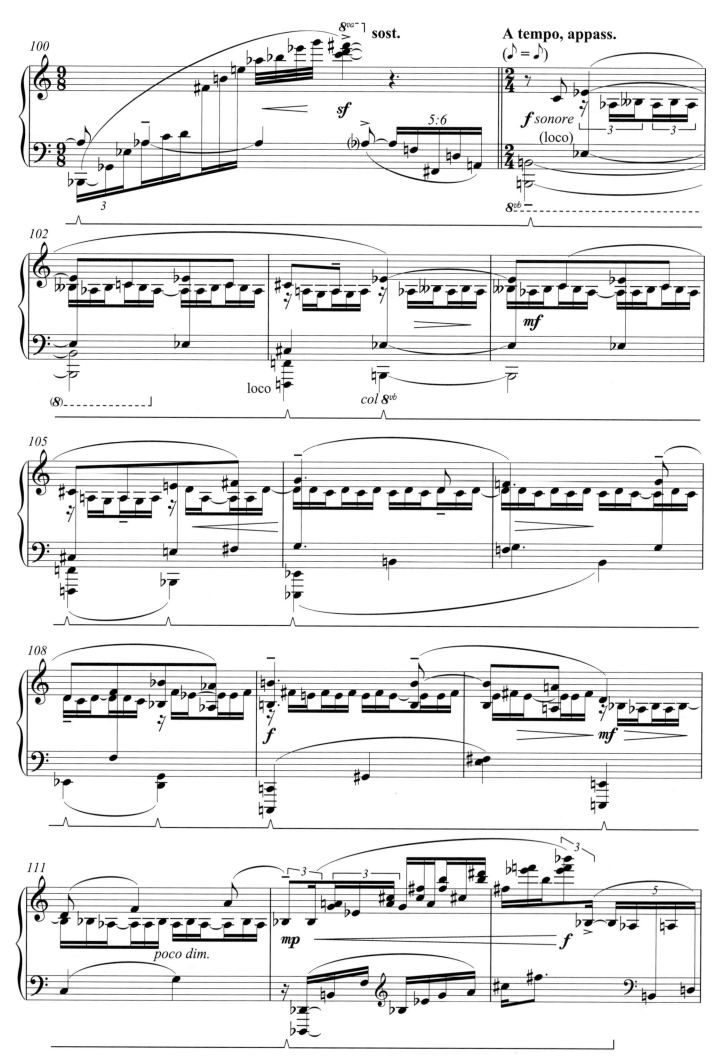

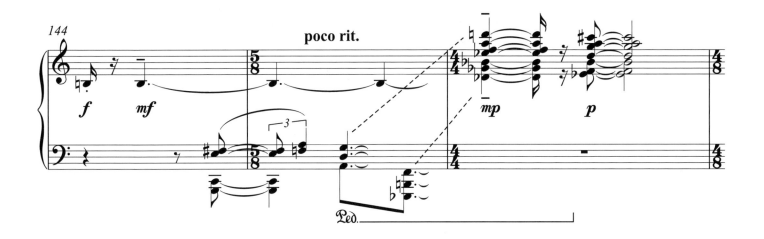

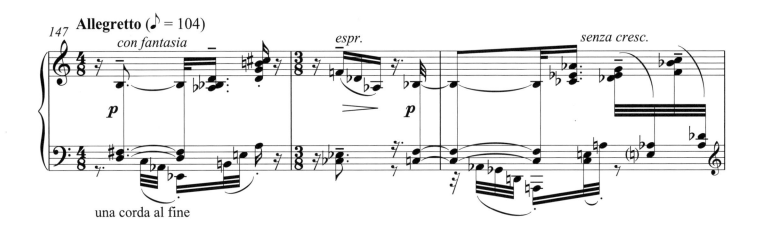

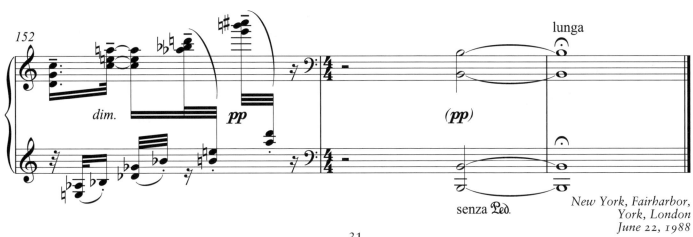

New York, Fairharbor,
York, London
June 22, 1988

For Sandra and Bill Charlap, 5 June 1993

Excursions

II. Andante lento

Richard Rodney Bennett

T HE 'Andante lento' is the central movement of *Excursions*, specially written for the 16-year-old Freddy Kempf, the BBC Young Musician of the Year of 1992, who had just won an award that included the commissioning of a work from a British composer. 'Richard Rodney Bennett was my No.1 choice', remembers Kempf, 'and I was delighted when he accepted. I loved all 3 movements — a perfect balance of classical and jazz, incredibly well-written, as you'd expect from a pianist. They were both challenging and satisfying pianistically. I particularly loved the sad bluesy feel of the middle movement.'

In this Andante, with its soulful motif developed with dexterity and given a contrasting central section of rippling despair, Richard would seem to be looking back on all those moody, downtown New York piano bars that so helped draw him across the Atlantic in the late Seventies. The memory of a lost love, perhaps even the one experienced at that time and never forgotten, would seem to suffuse every note.

If the Andante conjures thoughts of Richard in reflective mood, the jaunty syncopated movements that surround it and make *Excursions* such a satisfying whole bring to mind his boundless vitality and immense sense of fun.

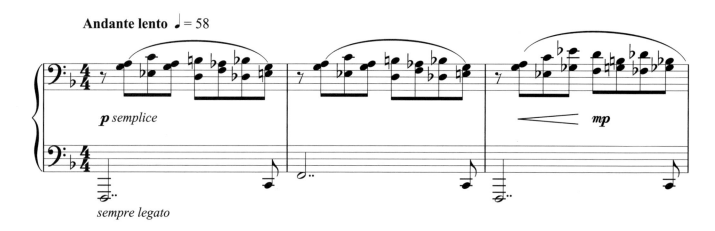

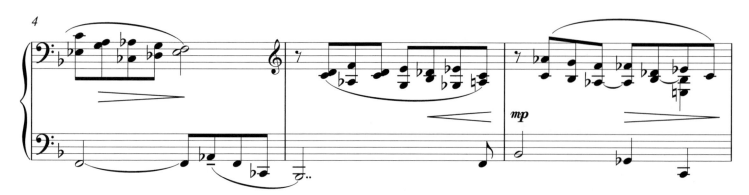

Partridge Pie
VIII. Eight Maids a-Milking

RICHARD was a pragmatic composer, always wishing to be of use. When from time to time he was asked to write pieces for young pianists, he did so delightedly. 'For such commissions', he commented on his own recording of them, 'I like to take a poem and base the different movements on the ideas it brings to mind.' *Partridge Pie*, written for pianists up to around Grade VI and based on the old rhyme *The Twelve Days Of Christmas*, is the best of several such projects.

'I wrote a piece of music about each of the different Christmas gifts in the poem', Richard explained. 'But it isn't a specifically Christmas piece. I called it *Partridge Pie* to give an idea of all the kinds of surprises it contains.' The short 'Eight Maids a-Milking' gives an amusing picture of the passion with which the maids are going about their work, suggesting a productivity level that would be wholly satisfactory to the Milk Marketing Board.

Other splendid vignettes include dramatic Scottish bagpipes (11 Pipers), an evocative misty landscape embellished with birdsong (4 Calling Birds) and the gentlest of salutes to Cy Coleman and the Great American Songbook (7 Swans).

Partridge Pie
VIII. Eight Maids a-Milking

Richard Rodney Bennett

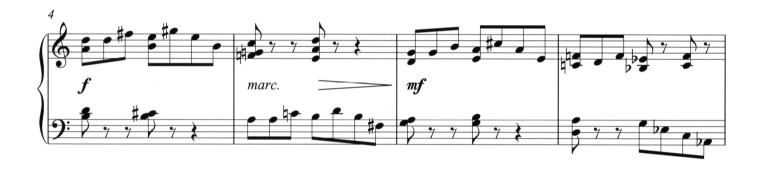

Memento

I is thought that the ancient Greeks used masks in performances of tragedies to contain emotions that would otherwise have been too painful. Similarly, perhaps, when asked to contribute to a memorial concert for Howard Ferguson, Richard resorted to all the formal techniques of his trade to help him cope. For he was not good at facing up to life's unhappinesses, preferring to exclude them rigorously from his mind, but this was something which, though very painful, his strong loyalty to old friends forced him to face.

'A rhapsodic little gem', writes the American pianist and conductor Scott Dunn of *Memento*, which, most movingly, he played at Richard's own memorial concert in London, thirteen years later at St Paul's Church, Covent Garden: 'It's based on a lovely tune derived from the scale tones in Howard Ferguson's name: H (B natural), A, D, F, E, G, 'S' (Es, E flat). Though the piece begins and ends with straightforward statements of the tune, in characteristic serial fashion Richard manipulates the tune with inversions, retrograde and retrograde inversion treatments. But, as usual, he uses that technique to create an effortless, quietly impassioned and wholly natural-sounding tonal character piece. It's a joy to play and quite beautiful.'

Memento

Richard Rodney Bennett

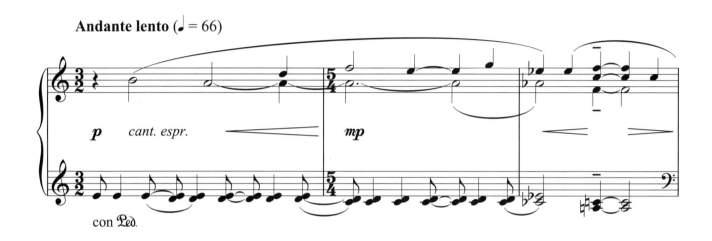

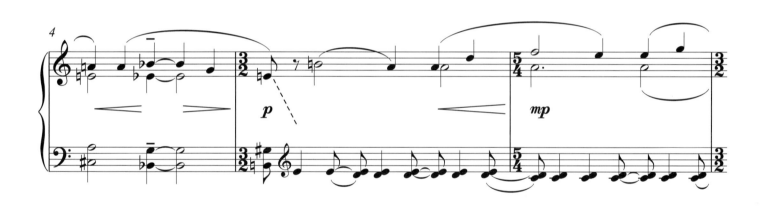

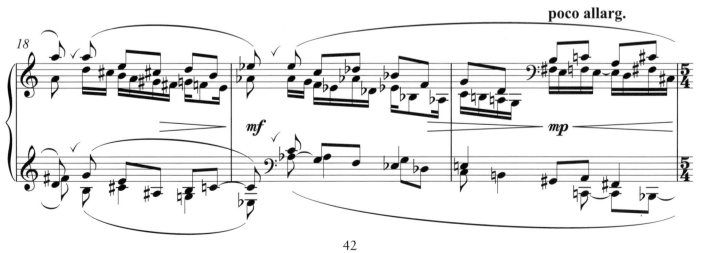

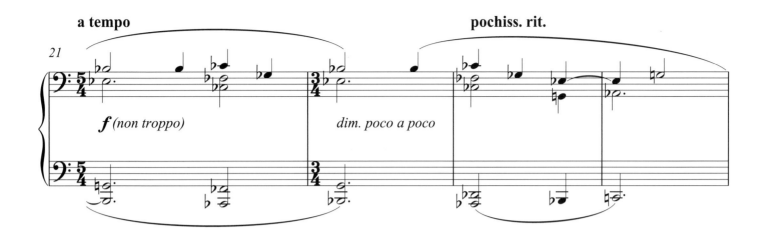

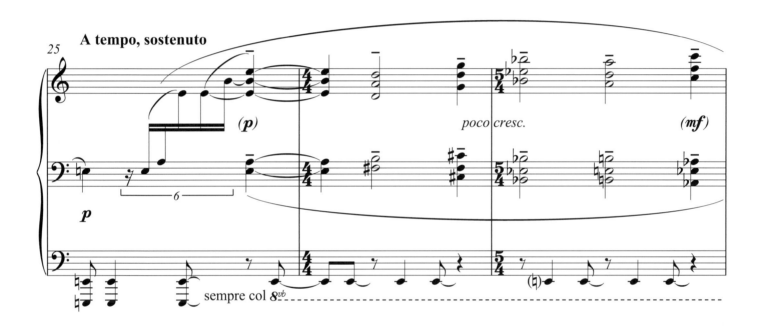

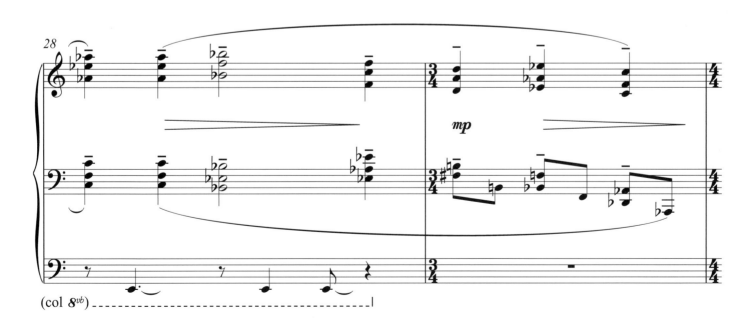

44

Little Elegy

Richard Rodney Bennett

RICHARD's last piano work, *Little Elegy*, comes from *Variations For Judith*, a collection of piano variations by different composers on the Bach-Stölzel aria 'Bist du bei mir' ('If you are with me, I will go gladly to death and to any rest'), presented to Judith Serota to mark the end of her long association with the Spitalfields Festival.

Richard had been resolutely disregarding signs of failing health for some time, but if he had any reservations about such a poignant song, he put them aside in creating this lyrical and impassioned piece. After its performances by Melvyn Tan at the Spitalfields and Cheltenham Festivals, the *Daily Telegraph*'s Ivan Hewett pointed out that while the other composers had been content to place 'a musical halo' round the song's delicate pathos, amplifying the hint of bells in the melody with chiming, softly-pedalled chords, Richard was the only one to break the mould, finding 'a rich, Great-American-Songbook pathos in the melody that no-one could have suspected'. And yet, somehow, in a feat of virtuosity, he had preserved the shape and delicacy of the original, 'like a bottled essence'.

Many of the strands of Richard's diverse life seem to come together in this deeply felt adieu.

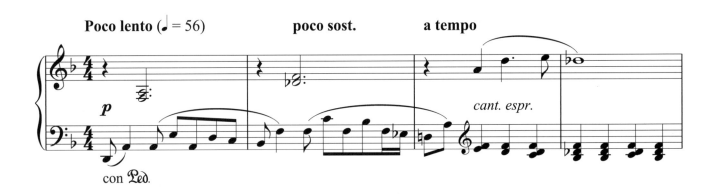

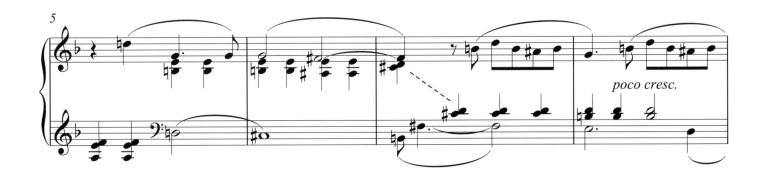

123456789

Bringing you the words and the music

All the latest music in print... rock & pop plus jazz, blues, country, classical and the best in West End show scores.

- Books to match your favourite CDs.

- Book-and-CD titles with high quality backing tracks for you to play along to. Now you can play guitar or piano with your favourite artist... or simply sing along!

- Audition songbooks with CD backing tracks for both male and female singers for all those with stars in their eyes.

- Can't read music? No problem, you can still play all the hits with our wide range of chord songbooks.

- Check out our range of instrumental tutorial titles, taking you from novice to expert in no time at all!

- Musical show scores include *The Phantom Of The Opera*, *Les Misérables*, *Mamma Mia* and many more hit productions.

- DVD master classes featuring the techniques of top artists.